table of contents

intro

affirmation one

the things we carry

reflection one

black woman?

you must bend, but don't break

affirmation two

why

reflection two

fruta

her(story)

affirmation three

ranting

this that (I am)

affirmation four

I delayed writing this for almost three years. I hesitated confronting the ugly parts of me since I already struggled to see the beauty I possessed. I let fear and uncertainty, along with the potential judgment from others subconsciously invalidate what I had to say and even who I was. I allowed suppressed feelings of rejection and all the heavy things I carried hide the light I was supposed to hold high. I allowed "no's", "not now's" and "why's" stifle the life of my dreams and then proceeded to accept a reality that paled in comparison. I let shame of imperfection disguise the scars and places in me that needed healing. I allowed this to linger for a long time in my life.

Broken and barely holding myself together, I decided to say yes to myself regardless of who hesitated. I decided to love myself more than anyone else could. It was then, I recognized that every dream that had been placed on the inside of me by the Creator would manifest. I considered the future of the generations that would come through my womb and the effect my life would have on them. I considered the people I loved.

Somewhere along this journey, I learned to find strength in all that I am. I am at peace and there's not one soul who could validate my existence, my value, and my royalty more than I. I learned there's power in. peace. The same power I had given away foolishly thinking someone else was more equipped to weld it. I learned the power was mine.

Writing helped me realize there was power all around and power within me. Power running through my veins, power in my pain, power in every tear that fell onto my cheek, power in prayers, power in my thoughts, power in every word written on a page. Power in telling pieces of my story and the things I learned along the way not for accolades or recognition, but simply to share in hopes that it would help someone else see their own power.

I realize how important my story is; my narrative and the one that is possible for my children and their children.

I push fear and doubt aside to take action re-gardless of per-ceived limitation because I know all of my needs are being met.

the things we carry

like happy weight in the beginning when affinity becomes *love*

like a seed that forms into a baby in 9 months, conceived of that *love*

like the emotional baggage received from what was once deep *love*

like a disease that eats away at open wounds continuing to believe in that *love*

like the voices of those around you saying who you can and can't be, is that *love?*

like a concealed weapon fired, never saw the damage coming from reciprocity of true *love*

like the confidence snatched from your being because you bet everything on *love*

like not being able to find your key to set you free from the reality of lost *love*

like the cross you bear when seeking spirituality to ease the grief of *love?*

like water on the head of ancestors in triple degree because you need that *love*

like a wad of crumbled cash in the double D's you keep *love*

like the world in all its gravity on one knee simply to be *love*d

How do you love yourself?

In what areas could you love yourself more?

Name 3 ways in which you will love yourself more completely this month.

black woman?

woman, what are those dark coils that crown your head?
they respond at their own will and dare to be tamed
they mimic her strength

how does her skin so golden, perfectly rise and fall over peaks
and valleys that form tantalizing curves?

curves that flow like milk from a coconut, like rivers over thighs,
hips and ass thick like honey
honey that leads to her treasures within, so sweet

her heart is made of gold
she loves fully although she encounters excuses for the full-
ness of love in return

she waits for the manifestation of it
and it comes, though not as she expects

it starts as a seed
then becomes a being that nourishes from her rich soil

she is still giving
and what she gets she can hold one day soon

she'll protect her love from past trauma, broken promises and
not being a woman who has been fully loved

no inhibitions
she will show up to fully love and
it is then she will be loved by something that comes from within

it starts from within

who is a black woman?

she can not be overlooked
she must be protected

her story is complicated
her prowess has been perfected through a long line of ancestors

her light,
it can't be dimmed

you must bend, but don't break.

I can remember a time thinking, "God, I'm such a great catch I can't understand why he doesn't feel the same way about me that I feel about him". I know there's a lot of women who have felt this way at least one time or another. You're upset because he won't commit to a relationship. He won't commit to a marriage. He won't even commit to actually answering your call. It happens and yeah, it sucks. First things first, for the man who won't commit to answering your call you might not want to bend at all, and especially don't bend over. You see, there's one fact that remains true no matter what anyone tells you; people do what they want to do. Keys to any relationship is reciprocity and balance. We all have our different baggage we carry around and so when you're faced with the issue of really feeling someone, but not feeling the terms they present there are 3 things you must do. 1) Ask yourself what value are they providing you in the relationship or interaction and does it match what you bring. 2) Ask them to explain the terms and then independently reflect on those terms. You have to respect who people are. In a healthy relationship, more than just your perspective is considered, more than just your perspective should be respected and more than just one perspective can be and often is accurate. 3) Be willing to compromise, but do not risk the core of who you are.

At the end of the day, YOU are the one constant in your own life and what good comes from pouring from an empty vessel or a vessel filled with things that don't belong? And if you ever find yourself asking, "where is this going?" It might not be going sis! That can be disappointing but don't attach someone's unwillingness to your self worth and it's okay to stand your ground and refuse conformity or not. Plus time always reveals the tough stuff. Be true to yourself. Be willing to grow and evolve and be flexible, but don't become so malleable that you lose the essence of who you are.

It is my responsibility to love myself. Loving myself fully, sets the tone for how others should love me.

why?

he asked, "why are you hiding?"
I asked, "what are you trying to see?"

you see, I hide, smile wide cause I learned this world
is a cold place to be
those trying to mine the depths of me to take for their
own blessing
fake friends see real joy and turn to enemies

he said, "peel back"
I said, "why?"
how come you wanna go so deep?

because the wall I built yields to layers of a woman
who doesn't want to be exposed to the disappointment
of continuity

or lack of that when things get too heavy
when you don't understand my needs
and I have to remind you that you're the one who
asked to see me

like a mirror, I see through them
those like you who proclaim love
I said, "what's you truth?"

I'll let you feel my surface
hesitant to let you be a conduit beneath, but you can
skim

I asked again, "why do you want to come into me?"

because people take what they want
they see what they need

they pillage and plunder
steal your light right from under….. you
then leave you to recover

I said, "What are you trying to see?"
what motivates your curiosity?
what's your decree?

We as women have many roles.

mothers
sisters
aunts
friends
daughters
wives
girlfriends
partners
CEO's
chefs
models
educators
lovers
nurturers

How do you define
yourself and why?

How do you show
up in your different
roles?

Are there ways in
which you desire to
shift in/out of these
roles? Why? How?

fruta

fruits of the spirit

fruit from the earth

fruits of my labor

fruit of my womb

you'll know a man by them

exotic, fresh, peeled, strange, yet full of life and ripe,

but you can't pick me

I chose to whom I give

peace of fruit

fruits of victory

my first fruits

because I bear them

fruitful

fruition

her(story)

Storytelling has been a centerpiece in cultures across the globe seemingly since the beginning of time. The telling of story educates, captivates, liberates and entertains. It weaves pieces of history together and is a bridge that connects generations with shared language.

I can remember my great-grandmother telling me her own stories since I was a child. I would look forward to coming home after school and listen to her tales of life as I braided her hair. She would often talk about being born in the south and moving to New York City and then eventually to Connecticut. She would talk about the farm she was raised on in North Carolina and the abundance of fruit and animals. She would talk about the many run-ins she had with racism and the evolution of being a black woman over the 90 years she lived on this earth. She would talk about the violence she witnessed and experienced over the years. She would talk about the power of making a person feel good about who they are even if it didn't look so good. She was the type to tell you how beautiful you were even if everyone in the room thought it to be the biggest lie ever told.

The theme throughout all her stories was she never chose silence. Whether through word or deed she stood up for what she believed to be right and from a very young age pushed me to tell my own stories.

To me she was and remains a hero. She is one big reason I'm here today. I didn't know it then but, it was Lillian who introduced story to me. It was my great-grandmother who let me know how important my voice and story is.

I am a visionary be-
cause I can see
without looking and
I don't let what "it"
looks like dictate
what I can see.

ranting

I know the feeling of wanting something great that
seems to be right out of your grasp. Being in the same
space as privilege isn't easy. I used to dream of going
to Yale. Not as an outsider or patient technician but,
exclusively. I can speak to my diverse background that
includes supervising a 125-bed residential substance
abuse treatment facility, leading a NYC Public School
and being CEO of my own company. Those things
certainly make me knowledgable. However, those ex-
periences alone are not representative of who I am
and what I can offer. Why do we place so much value
on accomplishments and accolades? Indeed those
things are important. Yet, what I find more appealing
about me is the fact that I love hard, that I have a spirit
that can soothe a raging storm, that I will stick by the
side of those I love when there is nothing left except
crumbling bricks to rebuild and I will come through
guns blazing if it ever gets real no hesitation. Sure I
went to Howard and Harvard and that speaks to my
tenacity and ambition but, have you ever eaten a meal
made with love when you didn't think you had any-
thing to eat? Have you ever had a friend that never left
your side or tell you the truth when no one else
would? Have you ever had a friend so free and spon-
taneous? Have you ever been in love on 5 different
continents? Have you ever had someone make you
rethink all you could be or simply say, "it's gonna be
okay" in a challenging time? Have you ever had
someone love you the best they could even when you
weren't your best self. Don't lose that.

this that (I am)

that diaspora
that rhythm,
that cuff,
that kinfolk,
that black skin,
that "this ain't enough"

that covenant
that promise
those riches
that scripture
that Nile
that river

that ivory
that ocean
that Zulu
that knuck
that buck
that beat of this drum

that drive
that "what's inside you?"
that "you can no longer hide you?"

I am an unstoppable Queen.

Reflection

_____

_____

_____

_____

_____

_____

_____

_____

_____

_____

_____

_____

_____

_____

_____

Made in the USA
Middletown, DE
21 August 2020